The Trial of Rattenfanger

Justine Cope

with poetry by Robert Browning &
Henry Wadsworth Longfellow

Beercott

The Trial of Rattenfanger
A play in one act

First Published in Great Britain in 2019 by Beercott Books.

Copyright: © Justine Cope 2019

ISBN: 978-1-9997429-8-0

Justine cope has asserted her rights to be identified as the author of this book.

Title is fully protected under copyright. All rights, including professional and amateur stage production, recitation, lecturing, public reading, motion picture, radio broadcasting, television and the rights of translation into foreign languages are strictly reserved.

A catalogue record of this book is available from the British Library.

No one shall make any changes to the play for the purpose of production. No part of this book may be reproduced, stored in a retrieval system, or transmitted in any form, by any means, now known or yet to be invented. This includes mechanical, electronic, photocopying, recording, videotaping, or otherwise, without the prior written permission of the publisher. No one shall upload this title, or part of this title, to social media websites.

Professional and amateur producers are hereby warned that title is subject to a licencing fee. Publication of this play does not imply availability for performance. Both amateurs and professionals considering a production are strongly advised to apply to the agent before starting rehearsals, advertising, or booking a theatre. A licence fee must be paid whether the title is presented for charity or gain and whether or not admission is charged.

Worldwide licence enquiries for this title should be directed to:
licensing@beercottbooks.co.uk.
Title subject to availability.

---

www.beercottbooks.co.uk

Beercott

ABOUT THE AUTHOR

Justine Cope is a Creative Arts and Drama Practitioner, Director and Lecturer in Education. Her passion for writing stems from her love of creativity and devising, scripting and directing drama, theatre and arts projects.

She works with numerous educational settings and arts organisations to design and deliver creative provision, in addition to being a Creative Director of Fusion Performance Arts, in Staffordshire.

Justine has written several award winning One Act Plays for Youth/Young Performers which have been performed as part of The All England Theatre Festival including 'Scratching the Surface' and 'From Ashes to Coals'.

ABOUT THE PLAY

'The Trial of Rattenfanger' is a one act play which uses a range of documentary sources, poetry and verse to explore the story of the Pied Piper. The piece presents possible solutions to the loss of 130 children from the town of Hamelin, Saxony, Germany as charted in the towns scriptures and depicted in the stained-glass window commissioned for Hamelin church in 1300, which was later destroyed by fire.

The play was first performed as part of the Tamworth Hastilow One Act Play Festival, at the Tamworth Assembly Rooms on 20th March 2015 with the following cast.

CHARACTERS

TOWN CRIER	Josh Moult
ARBITRATOR	Jonathan Bott
THE RATTENFANGER	Eleanor McFarlane
ANIKA	Beth Moult
ELSEBETH	Isabelle Foxall
FRIDA	Bettina Shepherd
OTTO	Dylan James
LIESL	Jodie Birks
GRETA	Zoe Hunter

Ensemble/Chorus of Villagers & Children

The images above show Hans Dobbertin's impression of the original window (destroyed by fire) in Hamelin church, and the window recreated using lighting gel for the original production by Fusion Performance Arts.

CHARACTERS

Town Crier

Arbitrator

The Rattenfanger

Anika

Elsebeth

Frida

Otto

Liesl

Greta

Ensemble/Chorus of Villagers & Children

AUTHOR'S NOTE

Casting is flexible and can be expanded to incorporate a large ensemble of chorus/villagers/children or rats!

The poetry offers opportunities for casts to enhance story telling through the use of physical theatre, dance or tableau.

Minimal properties are required to stage the production and scenes should be presented fluidly. However, it is essential to represent the church window which can be achieved through creation of a physical window or by projection.

Act 1 — THE TRIAL OF RATTENFANGER

OPENING

A group of children dressed in white enter ceremoniously with the RATTENFANGER, they form a tableau representative of the church window in Hamelin church. Three village females sit quietly praying.

TOWN CRIER: In the year of 1284, on the day of Saints John and Paul
By a piper, clothed in many kinds of colours,
130 children born in Hamelin were seduced,
and lost at the place of execution near the *Koppen*.

The RATTENFANGER who is clearly shackled is removed from the tableau; he is thrust forwards and the children and villagers disperse. A bright light appears from above, the ARBITRATOR appears: -

ARBITRATOR: You are the one they call Rattenfanger?

RATTENFANGER: I am known by many names, that is but one of them.

ARBITRATOR: Quite! And that is but one of the reasons you remain here.

RATTENFANGER: I remain here, as you chose to hold me against my will.

ARBITRATOR: Well, then are you ready to tell the truth about your crimes?

RATTENFANGER: I know not to what you refer? I have committed no crimes, I have merely served my duty, and for that am I to be shackled for eternity?

ARBITRATOR: Your shackles are bound by your own dishonesty Rattenfanger! If you choose to impart the truth about your actions, your chains will be removed, and you will be able to pass freely through.

RATTENFANGER: Pass freely through? I have stated my case time after time, and yet am still tethered like an animal. I have committed NO crimes, I am a loyal subject and have always served my masters. What am I accused of? What have I done? Am I to remain here, held against my will - without fair trial for an undisclosed crime?

ARBITRATOR: Do not mock me Rattenfanger, you know to what I refer! The Hamelin children, 130 innocents taken from their town. Why Rattenfanger? What led you to this unprecedented act of evil?

RATTENFANGER: Surely, he that knows everything, holds the answer to this question? I have withheld nothing from the world, therefore, I have nothing to repent for.

ARBITRATOR: He that knows everything will judge you in his own time Rattenfange, however, you must first explain your actions. The mortal world remains confused as many versions of events exis, only you can tell the truth about the Hamelin children.

RATTENFANGER: I have never hidden the truth, my story has been elaborated upon and told a thousand different ways! Am I also to be held responsible for the fictitious tales of others, unable to rest freely?

ARBITRATOR: The freedom you seek will be granted once the truth is established Rattenfanger. Hundreds of years have passed since the Hamelin children disappeared, yet the world still seeks answers, answers that you hold.

RATTENFANGER: Why do you seek my truth, when you place such emphasis on the accounts of others?

ARBITRATOR: Scriptures, pictures and poems attempt to provide plausible solutions, but only you can tell the real truth, Rattenfanger. Look down and ponder, see how the world sees you and then tell your truth - or be forever bound by your chains!

Act 1   THE TRIAL OF RATTENFANGER   13

The RATTENFANGER looks on. We are transported to Hamelin Town (as depicted in Robert Browning's poem).

The ARBITRATOR exits and the RATTENFANGER picks up his pipe and begins to pipe his way around the countryside merrily. A company of villagers are soon revealed and the RATTENFANGER exits.

MAYOR: Hamelin Town's in Brunswick,

VILLAGERS: By famous Hanover city;
The river Weser, deep and wide,
Washes its wall on the southern side;
A pleasanter spot you never spied;
But, when begins my ditty,
Almost five hundred years ago,
To see the townsfolk suffer so
From vermin, was a pity.

Three female villagers break away from the group and begin to pray./ and // indicates overlapping of speech.

FRIDA: Dear Lord it is now 100 years /since our children were taken away from us.

ELSEBETH: /Lord hear my prayer, it is some 300 years since //our children left the town.

ANIKA: //Lord above, I pray for our lost children, it is now 500 years since they were lost. I pray that our town will never be subjected to the pain, sorrow and disease spread by the black rat. *(The other villagers join in)* I pray that the sacrifices we made will protect us in the future and that our children continue to look down as angels of purity and peace. We pray that the terrible events that blighted our town are never repeated.....

ANIKA: We ask this in your name/ and vow to serve thee most faithfully. AMEN.

ELSEBETH: /we pray //you hear us dear lord – AMEN

FRIDA: //Oh Father hear our prayer – AMEN.

A child (OTTO) comes forward and addresses one of the women (FRIDA) - the other villagers move upstage.

OTTO: You were talking about the children, the Hamelin children?

FRIDA: Every year we pray for them, you must have heard the stories? They were taken 500 years ago, never to be seen again! The heart ripped from this town, and we must pray it never happens again.

OTTO: They were taken by The Rattenfanger, my Oma told me.

FRIDA: Your Gross Mutter told you about the Rattenfanger?

OTTO: It makes her very sad, she said that her Gross Mutter told her the story when she was very small, and that she was always frightened of being taken away by him.

FRIDA: Dear child, tis true enough that the Rattenfanger had a part to play in their disappearance, but that's only the tip of the tale. You know about the black rat? *(child shakes his head).* A dangerous creature, full of disease arrived in Hamelin; they multiplied and sullied our land. Soon our foods were contaminated and the children, the weakest of our town began to fall sick. Such a terrible plague, misery and pain the like you have never seen, and the rats they just grew and grew......

The villagers address the front

FRIDA: And they were everywhere!

ALL: Rats!

VILLAGER 1: They fought the dogs and killed the cats,
and bit the babies in the cradles,

VILLAGER 2: And ate the cheeses out of the vats,
and licked the soup from the cooks' own ladles,

VILLAGER 3: Split open the kegs of salted sprats,
Made nests inside men's Sunday hats,

ALL: And even spoiled the women's chats,
by drowning their speaking
with shrieking and squeaking
in fifty different sharps and flats.

The above turns into a choral speech the rats underscoring with rounds of squeaks.

OTTO: But was there no, solution, no cure?

FRIDA: The townsfolk begged and begged the Mayor for help, they knew the only way to stem the plague was to rid the town of the rats, he refused to listen, and feelings were running high.

CHORUS: At last the people in a body To the Town Hall came flocking:

ALL: 'Tis clear', cried they,

VILLAGER 1: Our Mayor's a noddy!

VILLAGER 2: And as for our Corporation shocking!

CHORUS: For now you must determine, what's best to rid us of our vermin! Rouse up, sirs! Give your brains a racking, or, sure as fate, we'll send you packing!

FRIDA: *(to OTTO)* An hour they sat in council,

MAYOR: It's easy to bid one rack one's brain -- I'm sure my poor head aches again, I've scratched it so, and all in vain.

ALL: Oh for a trap, a trap, a trap!

VILLAGER 2: Just as he said this, what should hap, at the chamber door but a gentle tap?

FRIDA: *(to OTTO)* That's when he arrived, a peculiar little man he was.

OTTO: The Rattenfanger?

FRIDA: Yes, the Rattenfanger.

VILLAGER 3: Come in, the Mayor cried – looking bigger.

CHORUS: And in did come the strangest figure! His queer long coat from heel to head, was half of yellow and half of red, And he himself was tall and thin, with sharp blue eyes, each like a pin, and light loose hair, yet swarthy skin, No tuft on cheek nor beard on chin, but lips where smile went out and in.

VILLAGER 2: He advanced to the council-table: Please your honours, said he...

RATTENFANGER: I'm able,
By means of a secret charm, to draw all creatures living beneath the sun, that creep or swim or fly or run,
the mole and toad and newt and viper;
and people call me the Pied Piper!

FRIDA: So desperate they were that they put their trust in the Rattenfanger, ignorant to the events that would unfold.

OTTO: Oma said that the town asked him to charm the rats away.

FRIDA: They did that, they thought that if the rats were gone the plague would disappear. They were naïve and didn't realise that the plague already had a hold on the place, but under *their* instructions the Rattenfanger started by culling the rats.

CHORUS: Into the street the Piper stepped,
Smiling first a little smile,
As if he knew what magic slept
In his quiet pipe the while;
Then, like a musical adept,
To blow the pipe his lips he wrinkled,
And green and blue his sharp eyes twinkled,
And ere three shrill notes the pipe uttered,
You heard as if an army muttered;
And the muttering grew to a grumbling;
And the grumbling grew to a mighty rumbling;
And out of the houses the rats came tumbling.
Great rats, small rats, lean rats, brawny rats,
Brown rats, black rats, grey rats, tawny rats,
Grave old plodders, gay young friskers,
Fathers, mothers, uncles, cousins,
Cocking tails and pricking whiskers,
Families by tens and dozens,
Brothers, sisters, husbands, wives --
Followed the Piper for their lives.
From street to street he piped advancing,
and step for step they followed dancing,

Act 1   THE TRIAL OF RATTENFANGER   17

    until they came to the river Weser
    Wherein all plunged and perished!
    Save one who, stood stout as Julius Caesar

OTTO: So, the Rattenfanger saved the town by getting rid of the Rats?

FRIDA: Oh, he charmed them rats right away, there's no doubt about that, but that's not where the story ends.

OTTO: Oma said that the townsfolk neglected to pay the Piper for his kindness, so he piped away their children!

FRIDA: Now child, I wouldn't go believing everything you hear. I don't doubt that they may have neglected to pay him, but it is just as likely that that because the rats carried the plague, the children were already infected with it, therefore there was only one thing left to do....

CHORUS: Once more he stepped into the street,
    And to his lips again
    Laid his long pipe of smooth straight cane;
    There was a rustling that seemed like a bustling
    Of merry crowd's jostling at pitching and hustling,
    Small feet were pattering, wooden shoes clattering,
    Out came the children running.
    All the little boys and girls,
    Tripping and skipping, ran merrily after
    The wonderful music with shouting and laughter.

FRIDA: The townsfolk could only look on as the children followed the Rattenfanger

OTTO: Didn't they try to stop them?

FRIDA: Maybe the children were so entranced that they could not hear their parent's pleas, or maybe the parent's accepted the ultimate sacrifice of losing their children to save the town from further plague? Either way they followed the Piper.

CHORUS: The Mayor was dumb, and the Council stood
    As if they were changed into blocks of wood,
    The children came merrily skipping by,
    And could only follow with the eye
    As the Piper turned from the High Street

To where the Weser rolled its waters
Right in the way of their sons and daughters!

When, lo, as they reached the mountain-side,
A wondrous portal opened wide,
As if a cavern was suddenly hollowed;
And the Piper advanced and the children followed,
And when all were in to the very last,
The door in the mountain-side shut fast.

OTTO: So, he took the children to save the town from the plague?

FRIDA: Maybe, some say he encased himself and the children inside the Koppen to save the town from plague, some say he took the children as payment for culling the rats.

OTTO: What really happened?

FRIDA: Now that is a question only the Rattenfanger himself can answer! The only truth we know is that no one ever saw the town's children again. Every year we remember and pray for them, and hope that such a tragedy never blights our town again.

The villagers disappear and RATTENFANGER is left alone with the Arbitrator again.

ARBITRATOR: You see Rattenfanger; your tale remains very much alive!

RATTENFANGER: You show me a rhyme about rats written almost 500 years after I left Hamelin and the rest is the tales of fishwives and washerwomen! What sort of evidence is this?

ARBITRATOR: It is evidence that history holds you responsible for the disappearance of the Hamelin children, as I said many scriptures, poems and songs have been written about you Rattenfanger. You could of course tell *your truth* and rewrite the History books.

RATTENFANGER: I should not have to explain myself – I have done nothing other than my duty!

ARBITRATOR: Then you must look deeper into the past Rattenfanger, maybe this account is the truth you hide

RATTENFANGER: What do you mean?.......

The RATTENFANGER watches as ELSEBETH enters with her daughter LIESL.

LIESL: Why do you still pray for the lost children Mutter?

ELSEBETH: Because they remain lost my dear, it was a tragedy the type of which must never be repeated.

LIESL: Herr Weiber says that *they* are the reason that no singing or dancing is allowed on the Bungelosenstrasse.

ELSEBETH: Herr Weiber should not be frightening you children with such tales, Liesl!

LIESL: He wasn't frightening us Mutter, we asked about the Bungelosenstrasse and he told us that it was the last place the children were seen.

ELSEBETH: That is true, it is said that the children were seen there shortly before they disappeared. Bungelosenstrasse means 'road without drums', because all fell silent when the children left.

LIESL: Herr Weiber said that the children were hypnotised by a Piper, dancing and singing, and that they followed him.

ELSEBETH: A Pied Piper I suppose?

LIESL: Yes Mutter, what does that mean?

ELSEBETH: A Piper adorned in a coat of many colours, look at the church window Liesl, there you see him, he is surrounded by the lost children.

LIESL: I don't understand Mutter, the Piper took them – he took them from their families and they were never seen again, why were they dancing? Were they happy to be taken?

ELSEBETH: No child, it was not a joyous dance, they were taken with the 'fire', such a terrible fever that made their bodies jerk so much it appeared as if they were dancing! Poor mites, how they suffered and what a price the town paid!

LIESL: What do you mean Mutter? Why did the town have to pay?

ELSEBETH: For causing the fever, you see it was their fault the children became sick. Times were hard, food was scarce and people starving. Poor weather meant that the Harvest was ruined, and we played the ultimate price.

LIESL: They let the children starve?

ELSEBETH: No, they fed them with rye bread which was all they had to offer, and due to the poor harvest the rye was contaminated with mould, soon the children, the weakest of the town became sick with the fire. You've heard the children's rhyme?

A children's game commences.

CHORUS 2: The rich man ate a bread of wheat; the poor made do with rye.
Summertime was tinged with rain and crops they failed to dry
We did not know the dangers, we did not see the wrong.
A cruel and painful poison, relieved only by a song.
So, dance my pretty children, dance until you drop
For the fires are burning, and they will never stop.

The chorus dance faster and faster until they drop to the floor.

CHILD 2: Why was it called the fire?

ELSEBETH: Some called it the 'Holy Fire', and some knew it as 'St. Anthony's fire'. The heat of the fever caused the children to burn up hence 'the fire'. Once the poison set in they suffered from violent fits, cramps and derangement. It must have been terrible to watch, it was like they were bewitched!

CHILD 2: So, what did they do?

VILLAGER 2: The only thing that they could, they appealed to the authorities for help. In some areas musicians were employed to play for sufferers, those afflicted danced and jumped uncontrollably with the pain and the music was said to ease their suffering. The townsfolk were in turmoil, more children were becoming ill, so the Mayor of Hamelin appointed a colourful piper to entertain the children, in the hope that it would minimise their suffering.

RATTENFANGER enters and begins to entertain the children:

RATTENFANGER: Amidst our people here is come
The madness of the dance.
In every town there now are some
Who fall upon a trance.
It drives them every night and day,
They scarcely stop for breath,
Till some have dropped along the way
And some are met by death. *(17th Century unnamed poem)*

The children dance to the music and eventually one at a time they fall. THE PIPER stokes the hair of a small child. The children disperse, and he is left alone again. The RATTENFANGER appears visibly touched by the scene.

ARBITRATOR: So Rattenfanger, is this the truth you are yet to tell?

RATTENFANGER: *(despondent)* I have told you, I have nothing to tell. What can I say that will change the course of the world?

ARBITRATOR: You cannot change the past Rattenfanger, but you can take charge of your own fate! Tell the truth and you will be judged in accordance with your actions, rather than by the way history has perceived you.

RATTENFANGER: I have no need or indeed wish to justify myself, your history lesson glorifies the suffering of those innocent of life, and I have no role to play in that.

ARBITRATOR: That's as maybe, but what about the needs of others, do they not need to know the truth Rattenfanger? – look again and see what they see.

The RATTENFANGER watches on again as FRIDA enters with a group of children.

GRETA: You said that you would tell us of the lost children, please tell us.

Children join in 'Yes please, please tell us' etc.

ANIKA: Ah such a special story, it happened many years ago and showed such innocence and bravery. You have heard of the children's crusade?

CHILD 2: Yes, our priest told us about it. Many children were chosen to journey to the holy land to give thanks to God and spread the word.

ANIKA: That's right, the innocence of children was seen to be a very powerful and precious commodity, therefore a group of children from our town were recruited to visit the holy land and promote Christianity.

GRETA: What happened to them?

ANIKA: A wonderful and magical guide was sent to lead them, he told them joyous tales of the promised land, entrancing them with every word. He was a skilled piper and played such beautiful music that the children were seduced by him! They sang and danced giving praise to the Lord as they travelled.

CHILD 3: Their Mutti's and Vatti's let them go?

ANIKA: My dear child it was a great honour for their children to be selected as servants to the Lord. However, yes, many parents tried to keep their children at home, bolting the doors and hiding them inside, but nothing could keep the children from following their vocation.

GRETA: I would never leave my Mutti and Vatti!

ANIKA: Times were very different then Greta, people could scarcely feed themselves and the guides were full of colourful stories, music and wonderful prophecies about the promised land, where food was plentiful and children would be treated like Kings and Queens. They not only placed their trust in the guide but also in God.

The RATTENFANGER enters and charms the children away to join him on his quest.

CHORUS: Is it fiction, is it truth?
    Children in the flower of youth,
    Heart in heart, and hand in hand,
    Ignorant of what helps or harms,
    Without armor, without arms,
    Journeying to the Holy Land!
    Who shall answer or divine?
    Never since the world was made
    Such a wonderful crusade
    Started forth for Palestine.
    Such an army, such a band,
    Over mountain, over main,
    Journeying to the Holy Land.

    How the days grew long and dreary,
    How their little feet grew weary,
    How their little hearts grew faint!
    But the dauntless leader said:

RATTENFANGER: 'Faint not, though your bleeding feet
    O'er these slippery paths of sleet
    Move but painfully and slowly;
    Other feet than yours have bled;
    Other tears than yours been shed
    Courage! lose not heart or hope;
    On the mountains' southern slope
    Lies Jerusalem the Holy!'

CHORUS: As a white rose in its pride,
    By the wind in summer-tide
    Tossed and loosened from the branch,
    Showers its petals o'er the ground,
    From the distant mountain's side,
    Scattering all its snows around,
    With mysterious, muffled sound,
    Loosened, fell the avalanche.
    Arbitrators, echoes far and near,
    Roar of winds and waters blending,
    Mists uprising, clouds impending,
    Filled them with a sense of fear,
    Formless, nameless, never ending.
Henry Wadsworth Longfellow

GRETA: So, they never made it to the Holy Land?

ANIKA: I am afraid not my dear, the journey was treacherous, and the children became exhausted quickly. Some fell along the way and the others were killed by the avalanche.

CHILD 3: What about their guide – the piper?

ANIKA: Perhaps he perished with them, perhaps he escaped, we will never know. The town was in mourning; we sacrificed our children and must live with that forever, so each year we continue to pray for them.

The villagers resume their original praying positions.

ARBITRATOR: You see Rattenfanger so many versions of events, so much remains unresolved, do you not feel a duty to tell the truth?

RATTENFANGER: Which 'truth' would you like me to tell? *(He watches on in frustration).*

ANIKA: Dear Lord it is now 100 years /since our children were taken away from us.

ELSEBETH: /Lord hear my prayer, it is some 300 years since //our children left the town.

FRIDA: //Lord above, I pray for our lost children, it is now 500 years since they were lost. I pray that our town will never be subjected to the pain, sorrow and disease spread by the black rat. *(The other villagers join in)* I pray that the sacrifices we made will protect us in the future and that our children continue to look down as angels of purity and peace. We pray that the terrible events that blighted our town are never repeated....

FRIDA: We ask this in your name/ and vow to serve thee most faithfully. AMEN.

ELSEBETH: /we pray //you hear us dear lord – AMEN

ANIKA: //Oh Father hear our prayer – AMEN.

ARBITRATOR: It is time Rattenfanger, you must let them know

Act 1   THE TRIAL OF RATTENFANGER

the truth. They think that *they* are responsible for the children's disappearance. Stand up and be judged for your actions.

RATTENFANGER: Don't you see no one is responsible! How can I be judged by 'he that knows everything' surely you know that *he* already knows the answer! He is responsible for the turning of the world, the stars in the sky and the fish in the sea. My role in this was merely to guide the children wherever they went, and where they went was ultimately his decision!

ARBITRATOR: And don't you see Rattenfanger, it is not he or I that judge you - it is history itself! My role is not to hold you to account for your actions, merely to show you how these have been presented throughout history and to find the truth.

RATTENFANGER: *(referring to the villagers)* To whom to they pray, and why do they feel responsible?

ARBITRATOR: They pray to you Rattenfanger.

RATTENFANGER: *(taken aback)* To me…but why?

ARBITRATOR: Because only you can ease their misery, where did you take the children Rattenfanger? The people need answers.

RATTENFANGER: I did not 'take them', they were given to me and therefore the answers they seek are not mine to give.

The Villagers surround RATTENFANGER in desperation

CHORUS: Rattenfanger, Rattenfanger, hear our plea
    Rattenfanger, Rattenfanger set them free
    Rattenfanger we repent, we know we did you wrong
    Rattenfanger, Rattenfanger come and pipe your song
    Rattenfanger, Rattenfanger name your price
    Rattenfanger, Rattenfanger we'll pay thee thrice
    Rattenfanger, Rattenfanger listen to our prayer
    Rattenfanger, Rattenfanger, release them from your lair!

RATTENFANGER: STOPPPPP! I beg you… please stop! I will answer your questions.

ARBITRATOR: You confess Rattenfanger? You admit your role in these crimes?

RATTENFANGER: I confess to taking the children, not to committing a crime.

FRIDA: You took them to the cave?

ELSEBETH: You played for them in eternal dance?

ANIKA: You led them to the holy land?

RATTENFANGER: Yes, yes,yes.

ARBITRATOR: Well which?

RATTENFANGER: All of the above and more, I take the innocents and lead them to their final resting place, that is my role – a vocation bestowed upon me by a force greater than thou.

ARBITRATOR: Elaborate, Rattenfanger what vocation, what force do you speak of.

RATTENFANGER: *(taunting the ARBITRATOR)* I am a beacon of shining light, I pipe each morning, day and night
In times of trouble, strife and fear, just call my name I will appear.
The guide of many and master of few, ethereal in all I do
Are you blind, cannot you see? My vocation sits higher than thee.

ARBITRATOR: You are talking in riddles Rattenfanger.

RATTENFANGER: Don't waste my time with petty discourse, I answer only to a higher force.
My duty is clear throughout this plane, to spare God's children from undue pain.
And guide them gently without haste, towards their final resting place.
You hold me here against his will, yet the key to heaven I hold still.
My work on earth is not yet done; so, pray, release me to the sun.
For my master I must serve, and guide the innocents as they deserve.
To take their places in a higher sphere, safe from illness, harm and fear.

Act 1   THE TRIAL OF RATTENFANGER

ARBITRATOR: Finally, Rattenfanger an attempt to explain your actions.

RATTENFANGER: As I said before, the answers you sought were not mine to give. You accused me of crimes, and therefore I stated my innocence. Not once did you consider my actions may have determined by the force responsible for our very existence. Whilst the history you speak of has been manipulated to depict me as a child catcher, a villain, a murderer.

ARBITRATOR: Then why did you not take action to defend yourself?

RATTENFANGER: Because there is nothing to defend, the answers were always in front of you - open to all to see?

ARBITRATOR: And pray, where does one find these answers you speak of?

RATTENFANGER: *(he points to the window)*. My portrait sits within Hamelin Church surrounded by the children you speak of, do you really think I would be enshrined in coloured glass had I been responsible for harming such innocents? It is the highest reverence to be to be immortalised in the house of the Lord!

ARBITRATOR: The town commissioned the window to honour you?

RATTENFANGER: As I said, the highest accolade one could ever receive is to reside in the Lord's house.

ARBITRATOR: Rattenfanger, now I bow to you *(he removes the shackles)* you are indeed your master's most obedient servant. A great injustice has been served upon you, you are of course free to pass through.

RATTENFANGER: I do not wish to pass through, my duty here is not complete. I must to remain here for eternity, watching over the lost children of Hamelin. That is the promise I made to my Master, and my duty I will serve readily.

The RATTENFANGER is removed from his shackles and he and the company form a tableau in front the church window.

The curtain falls.

Also by Justine Cope

Scratching The Surface

A one-act play for youth groups.

ISBN: 978-1-9997429-6-6

Cast: 18 – flexible casting including 2 adults, doubling possible.

Scenes: set in various locations in a bunker. Simple requirements for each location, ideal for festivals etc.

Running time: ~ 45 mins

Set in an underground bunker, we follow a group of young apocalyptic 'survivors' with dreams of urban exploration as they delve into the past to make sense of the future. They are guided by two adults referred to only as 'The Wise'. But who are the Wise and are they hiding something? And what of Nostradamus and the quatrains? Do they really hold the key to the downfall of the Relics (Adults) and the success of the New World?

Winner 'Best Original Play', Tamworth Hastilow One Act Play Festival, 2017

www.ingramcontent.com/pod-product-compliance
Lightning Source LLC
Chambersburg PA
CBHW071918070526
44583CB00016B/2044